William Stang

Germany's debt to Ireland

William Stang

Germany's debt to Ireland

ISBN/EAN: 9783337728199

Printed in Europe, USA, Canada, Australia, Japan

Cover: Foto ©ninafisch / pixelio.de

More available books at **www.hansebooks.com**

GERMANY'S

DEBT TO IRELAND

BY

REV. WILLIAM STANG, D.D.

FR. PUSTET,
Printer to the Holy See and the S. Congregation of Rites.

FR. PUSTET & CO.,
New York & Cincinnati.
1889.

CHAPTER I.

DURING the coming month of July (1889), the city and Diocese of Würzburg will celebrate with solemn rites and splendid festivities the twelfth centenary of the introduction of Christianity into Franconia by Irish Missionaries and Martyrs. The attention of the whole Christian world will again turn towards the "Isle of Saints," and gratefully recall the blessings which Erin, in her days of glory, bestowed on Continental Europe. Catholic Germany, in particular, will resound with the praises of those Sain ts and Apostles, who evangelized and civilized her barbarian ancestors. Germans, who are by nature grateful, have always acknowledged their religious and literary indebtedness to Ireland. One thousand years ago, the learned Monk, Ermenrich Von Reichenau, remarked to the Abbot of St. Gall: "How could we ever forget the Isle of Erin, from whence the Sun of faith, the radiance of so great a light has risen for us."

A thousand years of strange and sad changes have not cooled the warmth of gratitude in German hearts towards Ireland.

In the month of April, 1844, the leaders of Catholic Germany presented an address to the Irish Liberator, Daniel O'Connell, in which they said :

"It would, indeed, be divesting ourselves [the people of Germany] of all human sentiments, if we were not to entertain the deepest and sincerest sympathy for the ill-treated people of your isle, sighing under the yoke, and still reeking from the streams of shed blood. But want of sympathy on our part would, moreover, involve the blackest ingratitude. *We never can forget to look upon your beloved country as our mother in religion, that already, at the remotest periods of the Christian era, commiserated our people, and readily sent forth her spiritual sons to rescue our pagan ancestors from idolatry, at the sacrifice of her own property and blood, and to entail upon them the blessings of the Christian faith.* They thus have made us their, and their nation's, spiritual children, and laid up a store of merits for the people of Ireland, which only base indifference and want of all good feeling could be unmindful of, and which just now presents itself the more vividly to our memory, *the more we behold the native land of those faithful apostles delivered* over to undeserved misfortune by injustice."

When Germany sat in darkness and in the shadows of death, "Ireland was the ' seat of a flourishing Church,' abounding in the fruits of sanctity, learning and zeal." The old world with its wealth and wisdom was passing from the face of the earth, when that blessed Island in North had become "the store-house of the past and the birth-place of the future." The Religion which Patrick brought had taken a firm hold of the land and entered into the flesh and blood of the people so as to become their very life.

"For several centuries," says Father Thebeand, "after St. Patrick the island was the 'Isle of Saints,' a place midway between heaven and earth, where angels and saints of heaven came to dwell with mere mortals."

We recall the classic words of Dr. Doellinger regarding the period in which Ireland sent her heroic sons to evangelize the pagan nations of the Continent : "During the 6th and 7th centuries the Church of Ireland stood in the full beauty of its bloom. The spirit of the Gospel operated amongst the people with a vigorous and vivifying power ; troops of holy men, from the highest to the lowest ranks of Society, obeyed the counsel of Christ, and forsook all things, that they might follow him. There was not a country of the world, during the period, which could boast of pious foundations or of religious communities equal to those that adorned this far distant island. Among the Irish, the doctrines of the Christian religion were preserved pure and entire, the names of heresy or of schism were not known to them ; and in the Bishop of Rome they acknowledged and venerated the Supreme Head of the Church on earth, and continued with him, and through him with the whole Church, in a never interrupted communion. The schools in the Irish

cloisters were at this time the most celebrated in all
the West. Whilst almost the whole of Europe was
desolated by war, peaceful Ireland, free from the
invasions of external foes, opened to the lovers of
learning and piety a welcome asylum. The strangers,
who visited the island, not only from the neighboring shores of Britain, but also from the most remote
nations of the Continent, received from the Irish people the most hospitable reception, gratuitous enter-
tainment, free instruction, and even the books that
were necessary for their studies. Thus in the year
536, in the time of St. Senanus, there arrived at
Cork, from the Continent, fifteen monks, who were
led thither by their desire to perfect themselves in
the practices of an ascetic life under Irish directors,
and to study the Sacred Scriptures in the school established near that city. At a later period, after
the year 650, the Anglo-Saxons, in particular, passed
over to Ireland in great numbers for the same lauda-
ble purposes. On the other hand, many holy and
learned Irishmen left their own country to proclaim
the faith, to establish or to reform monasteries in
distant lands, and thus to become the benefactors of
almost every nation in Europe."

Charity is diffusive; its nature is to expand and
to communicate itself to others. Animated with
the purest zeal for the conversion of souls; burning
with the holiest desire of bringing the blessings of
their faith to others, the sons of St. Patrick left their
sweet and blessed country to go into the whole
world and to preach the Gospel to every creature.

St. Bernard, in his "Life of St. Malachy," remarks : "From Ireland, as from an overflowing stream, crowds of holy men descended on foreign countries." This deep-seated love of evangelizing has been graphically sketched by the Count de Montalembert : "A characteristic still more distinctive of the Irish monks, as of all their nation, was the imperious necessity of spreading themselves without, of seeking or carrying knowledge and faith afar, and of penetrating into the most distant regions to watch or combat paganism. This monastic nation, therefore, became the missionary nation *par excellence*. While some came to Ireland to procure religious instruction, the Irish missionaries launched forth from this island. They covered the land and the seas of the west. Unwearied navigators, they landed on the most desert islands ; they overflowed the Continent with their successive immigrations. They saw in incessant visions a world known and unknown to be conquered for Christ." Who has not heard or read of St. Brendan, the Irish sailor-monk, whose "fantastic pilgrimages into the great ocean, in search of the earthly Paradise, and of souls to convert" have exercised a religious charm over the Christian imaginations for twelve centuries? The account of his wonderful voyages was one of the first books printed in the German language. "For the Irish," says Wallafried Strabo, "the habit to immigrate has become their second nature."

Whilst the British would not cross the narrow span of water to bring the blessing of faith to Ireland, the Irish, after embracing the doctrine of the Crucified, would traverse every sea and country to carry the Gospel to heathen nations.*

Probably no other nation of the Continent owes so much to the missionary zeal of the Irish monks as Germany; no other country has been so abundantly blessed with the illustrious lives of Irish Saints as Germany. To-day, over one hundred and fifty Irishmen are invoked as patron saints in different parts of Germany. Among the earliest of the Irish missionaries whose names are held in pious remembrance were Fridolin, Columbanus, Gall, Sigisbert, Trudpert, Kilian, Colonat, Totnan, Virgilius and Disibod.

---

* The Irish not only penetrated the inhospitable and uncultivated parts of the Continent, we find them even on the shores of America as early as the eighth century. Grave historians admit that the Irish discovered America seven hundred years before Christopher Columbus colonized that portion of America now known as North and South Carolina, Georgia and East Florida. Gndlief Gndlaugsan, a Norse navigator, who landed here in the beginning of the eleventh century, found the people speaking Irish, and in the Sagas the country is called " Ireland-it-Mikla," that is great Ireland.

CHAPTER II.

THE first Irish Saint we meet on German soil is Fridolin, "the traveller," the son of an Irish king. He was born, in all probability, within the life-time of St. Patrick. In his early youth, Fridolin consecrated himself to God, and renouncing all earthly riches, looked and sought for the treasures of heavenly wisdom. After long and arduous studies he devoted himself to the service of God in the priesthood. He was gifted with a wonderful power of sacred eloquence, and soon won the admiration and loving enthusiasm of the people in cities and towns through which he travelled, preaching the word of God. Soon, however, Fridolin remarked within himself the presence of a dangerous enemy of his salvation. He felt himself inclined to vain glory and a desire to be praised and flattered. He saw the remedy for his rising passion in flight. He courageously left his beautiful country, and passing over to France, entered the monastery of St. Hilary at Poitiers where the monks, recognizing his learning and zeal, presently elected him their abbot. With the aid of King Clovis he rebuilt the church of St. Hilary, and there translated the relics of the saint. His great Patron appeared to him with the information that his work was not to end in France, but that God had destined him for another country and another nation. He told him to leave his work at Poitiers in the hands of his two nephews, who had followed him from Ireland to take some of the relics from the church (St. Hilary's), and to go to Alemania where, in the midst of a large river, he would find an island that the Lord had selected as the term of his missionary journeys. Fridolin obeyed the heavenly summons and quitted the land he had learned to love. So intense was his veneration for his Patron that on his wanderings and his searchings after the promised island, he founded monasteries and churches in honor of St. Hilary. We mention here the Monastery of Helera on the Moselle, a church of St. Hilary in Lorraine, and the church of St. Hilary in Strassburg. Finally he discovered the island on the upper Rhine, now known as the island of Saeckingen, above Basle, at the foot of the Black Forest, between Baden and Switzerland. Fridolin's heart leaped with joy as he set foot on the picturesque little isle, placed like a sparkling jewel on the bosom of the majestic river.

While he was seeking a suitable place for a chapel, the inhabitants noticing the behaviour of the stranger, and taking him for a spy or robber, seized him and after a cruel flogging, drove him from the isle. Fridolin returned to king Clovis from whom he obtained a letter granting him the isle, and threatening with capital punishment every one who would obstruct his taking possession of the land.

The inhabitants received him respectfully, this time, and helped him to build a church, monastery, school and convent. Idolatry and superstition were soon banished forever from Saeckingen and peace and prosperity blessed the isle and its inhabitants. Fridolin died in the fame of great sanctity on March 6th, about the year 550, and was buried in his own church. Among the many miracles which attested his spotless life and holy mission to the Alemani ; we mention the raising of a dead person to life and the changing of the Rhine in its course near Saeckingen. Fridolin first carried the lamp of faith into the heathen darkness of the Black Forest. His religious establishments became the celebrated nurseries of Christian civilization, and the monks of the monastery he had founded became the renowned teachers and religious instructors of the neighboring districts. To the present day, Fridolin's memory is held in benediction by the people of the upper Rhine, and story and legend have twined many a fragrant flower around that blossoming tree which the hand of God thus transplanted from the garden of the Irish church to grace the borders of Germany's noblest rivers and to give shade and rest to weary pilgrims on their journey towards eternity. St. Fridolin is presumably the first child of St. Patrick who gazed on the river Rhine.

CHAPTER III.

COLUMBANUS whose immortal fame outshines that of all his contemporaries and throws a lasting glory on the history of his time, was born of noble parents in the province of Leinster, in 535. His early education was entrusted to a learned and holy man, named Sinell. Columbanus was of great personal beauty, and in consequence, was exposed to many temptations which he struggled resolutely to overcome first by the study of the Scriptures, next by leaving his native land.

He entered the cloisteral halls of Bangor where hundreds of sainted monks served God devoutly in prayer, study and manual labor, under one of Ireland's brightest saints and scholars, Abbot Comgall. Columbanus was then twenty-five years old. In the course of time he became a zealous monk and ornament of the monastery. But, in his calm retreat, a voice kept constantly ringing in his ears : "Go out of thine own country, and from thy father's house, into the land which I will show thee." Despite the loving entreaties of Comgall to remain at Bangor, he persisted in his resolution to depart. At last, in 589, Columbanus received the Abbot's consent and blessing, and with twelve monks went forth upon his mission. Before embarking at Belfast, they prostrated themselves for the last time on their native soil and recommended themselves in prayer to to merciful guidance of God.

After a prosperous voyage they landed in France where a wide field opened before the priestly zeal of Columbanus. He first travelled through the country, preaching penance to those especially who had been baptized Christians, but who were fast relapsing into paganism. He then took up his residence with his companions first at the old castle of Annegray, then at Luxeul, in the Franche-Comté where they led a simple and austere life like to the Fathers of the Desert. Columbanus presently separated himself from his community and plunged into the forest that he might hold closer communion with God. Then the wild animals, as his biographer Jonas, informs us, would come at his call, the birds would playfully fly about him or confidently alight on his shoulders. A squirrel which knew him well would jump from the tree-tops and hide itself in the folds of his cowel. A raven became so attached to him that, at his order, it brought back his glove which it had roguishly carried away. Once he drove a bear from a cavern which he chose for his cell; at another time, he took from the jaws of a bear a dead stag whose skin served to make shoes for his monks.

We know from the lives of other saints that man intimately united in grace with God may obtain the privilege originally granted to our first parents to exercise a powerful influence and control over nature and the beasts of the earth. The blood of the early martyrs softened the rage of tigers and leopards. A wild bear which the day previous had devoured two gladiators in the ampitheater, was let loose, on the same spot, against St. Andronikus, but the ferocious animal would not touch the saint; it lay down peacefully and reverently kissed the feet of Andronikus. For sixty years a raven daily carried bread to the hermit, St. Paul, in the desert, and when he died two lions came and dug his grave. Need we wonder, if the wild animals became the servants and friends of St. Columbanus, who was so closely united with God?

Columbanus composed a book of rules and regulations for his monks at Luxeul. Some of his statutes appear to us rather harsh. One rule, f. i., ordained that the monk should go to bed so tired as to fall asleep on the way, or rise before he had slept enough. But we should remember with Count de Montalembert that "it is at the cost of this excessive and perpetual labor that the half of Gaul and of ungrateful Europe has been restored to cultivation and to life."

Columbanus had devoted twenty years of life in France to the reformation of its kings and people, when the wicked king, Theodoric, banished him and his Irish companions from the country forever.

It had always been his ambition and inclination to preach the gospel to heathen nations. His persecu-

tors enabled him to fulfill his holy desire ; he determined to evangelize the pagan Alemani.

With this intention he proceeded to Mentz where
Bishop Leonisius gave him the necessary provisions
for his journey. He ascended, with his countrymen,
the river Rhine, and came to Lake Zürich. He took
up his abode in Tuggen. The inhabitants were cruel
idolaters, and worshipped, as their chief god, Woden.
The Irish missionaries instructed them in the rudiments of the Christian religion and taught them to
adore the one true God in three persons.

One day Columbanus saw the natives around a
large vessel of beer, which they were to offer in sacrifice to Woden. At his approach the vessel burst
asunder and the foaming liquid ran hissing over the
ground. With all the impetuosity of his Irish tem-
per he burned their pagan temples, smashed their
gilded idols, and cast their brazen images into the
lake. But when his companion, St. Gall, set fire to
their sacred groves, the pagans became so enraged
that they determined to kill the zealous monk and to
scourge St. Columbanus. Shaking the dust from
his feet, he pronounced a woe upon the people who
had wilfully spurned the grace of conversion, and
went with Gall to Arbon, a christian settlement near
Lake Constance. The parish priest, Willimar, received the Irish missionaries kindly. He first led
them into his chapel for prayer, and gave them the
hospitality of his house. They sat down to a German dinner, during which St. Columbanus ordered
his disciple to read a passage from Holy Scripture

and to open the hidden meaning of the Divine Word.
St. Gall did all this with such simplicity, and yet
with such eloquence, learning and unction, that
Father Willimar was greatly astonished at the re-
markable erudition of his Irish guest, and even moved
to tears at his earnestness and sincere piety. He
prevailed on the missionaries to stay with him for
seven days. Willimar procured a boat which carried
them across Lake Constance to *Bregenz*. Here, in
this ruined city, they found the Church of St. Aurelia, once a Christian, but now a pagan temple.
They examined the surroundings and were pleased
with the location. And well they might be. The
country around Lake Constance baffles all description. The broad sheet of water, now fringed with
blooming meadows and smiling vineyards, must,
even in a less cultivated condition, have presented a
picture of singular beauty, set off by the snowy
mountains of Switzerland and the Tyrol in the near
distance. Adelaide Procter opens her celebrated
poem, "A Legend of Bregenz," with these rosy
lines :

> " Girt round with rugged mountains,
>   The fair Lake Constance lies ;
> In her blue heart reflected,
>   Shine back the starry skies.
> And, watching each white cloudlet
>   Float silently and slow,
> You think a piece of heaven
>   Lies on our earth below."

On the banks of this lovely lake St. Columbanus
and his disciples built their cells, close to the church

desecrated by idolatry and superstition. The natives had once been converted to the Christian faith, but relapsed into paganism. Columbanus made it known among them that he would reconsecrate the church to the service of God. Through curiosity the people came together in large crowds to see the strangers and to witness the solemn rites. Columbanus bade St. Gall, who spoke German fluently, preach a sermon to them. The eloquent Irish monk exhorted the people to renounce the follies of paganism and to return to their God and to his divine son Jesus, who had come into this world in order to redeem man and to open to him the gates of heaven. At the close of his discourse St. Gall tore down the idols from the walls of the church and flung them into the lake. Many were converted and confessed their sins, others left the church, filled with rage over the destruction of their false gods. Then the ceremony of Reconsecration began. The account which the old biographer gives is most interesting to a catholic in the 19th century; for the Rite is essentially the same as that in use on similar occasions at the present day in Boston or Chicago. St. Columbanus blessed water and with it sprinkled the walls of the church, and whilst the clergy walked in procession round the building, singing psalms, he rededicated it to God. Invoking the Holy Name, he anointed the altar, placed relics of St. Aurelia in it, and covered the table of the altar with white linen and then said Mass on it. When the solemnity was ended, the people returned to their homes with great joy.

Columbanus remained at Bregenz with his companions for three years, leading a cenobitical life. As the inhabitants were rather selfish, the monks were obliged to live on the wild birds of the forest and fish from the lake. They planted a garden and soon had vegetables for a variety.

The Priest, before baptizing, exorcises the child and takes from Satan whatever power he claims over it. Thus, in the conversion of nations, the Church had to drive Satan from his unlawful possessions and destroy the power which he exercised over the people. The old historian has preserved a striking illustration of this truth in the following narrative:

One night St. Gall went out to the lake to catch some fish for the sustenance of Columbanus and his disciples. As he was seated in his boat, watching his nets and saying his prayers, he heard the Demon of the neighboring mountains call for his companion in the depth of the lake: "Arise and help me to chase away those strangers who have expelled me from my temple, and have demolished my images and have won the people over to themselves." The Demon of the waters replied: "Behold, here is one of them upon the waterside whose nets I have tried to destroy, but I have never succeeded. Always absorbed in prayer, he never sleeps." When Gall heard this, he signed himself with the sign of the cross and then cried out: "In the name of Jesus Christ, I command you to leave these regions without daring to injure any one." St. Gall immediately returned to the shore and notified his mas-

ter of the occurrence. Columbanus had the bells
rung to assemble his brethren in the church for divine
service. And just before commencing the singing
of psalms, they heard the furious yells and infernal
shrieks of the demons echoing from the mountains
as they fled in dismay like a defeated army.

This story may appear somewhat incredible to the
Christian of the nineteenth century ; but he must bear
in mind that all the provinces of creation are divided
into two kingdoms, one of light, the other of darkness. (Gœrres.) The latter is waging a continual
war against the kingdom of light. Diabolical power
in its struggle against light, can, with the permission
of God, produce extraordinary phenomena, or, as
St. Thomas puts it, "the demons can produce all
those changes in physical substances of which they
are capable, according to their natural qualities."
(I., 114, 4.)

St. Columbanus did not find at Bregenz that peace
and solitude in which he desired to close his troubled
life. The inhabitants grew daily colder towards him,
and finally came to look upon him with suspicion as
an intruder and disturber of peace. Two of his monks
who had been falsely accused of stealing cows were
slain in an ambuscade, and his own life was in real
danger. "We have found a golden cup," he exclaimed bitterly, "but it is full of serpents."

In the seventy-ninth year of his age, he took his
staff and summoned the monks for departure to
Italy. St. Gall was laid up with a heavy fever ; he
entreated his master to excuse him from undertaking

the journey. But Columbanus, suspecting that Gall had grown too fond of the place, and was now feigning sickness in order to remain, said to the suffering monk : "Since thou wilt separate thyself from me, I debar thee, as long as I live, from saying mass."

Crossing the Alps, Columbanus founded in Italy the monastery of Bobbio, which he governed but one year. When he felt the approach of death, he left Bobbio and sought a still deeper seclusion in a cavern on the opposite shore of the Trebbia, where he passed his last hours in fasting and prayer. And thence on November 21, 615, God took unto Himself the great soul of Columbanus.

Though he spent only three years of his fruitful life on German soil, yet he has left abundant evidence of his apostolic zeal, and the fragrance of his virtues still lingers around beautiful Bregenz. A model monk, a fiery apostle, a distinguished author and defender of his faith, an able poet, and above all, a great saint is Columbanus, of whom a writer says : "Wonderful was the sanctity of Columbanus. Taught by the Holy Spirit, he established the monastic rule, and was the first who gave it to the Gauls. On earth he was distinguished for the miracles which God wrought through him ; and the virtues of his work shone forth as brightly as the stars of the firmament."

CHAPTER IV.

ST. GALL.

FIRST and foremost among the disciples of the great Columbanus stands St. *Gallus* or *Gall*, whose life is so identified with his master's that we have given a partial account of it in relating the history of Columbanus. Gall received his education at Bangor under him whom he followed as missionary to France and Alemania and with whom he would have gladly persevered to the end, had not an all-wise Providence decreed otherwise. God permitted him to be separated from his father and guide and to bear the heavy cross of ill-deserved reproaches; to be charged with faithlessness and hypocrisy by him whom he had loved so devotedly and served so faithfully and to be forbidden the heavenly joy of the daily celebration of mass. It is consoling to our human weakness to see that even saints may misunderstand each other.

Sick as he was, Gall would not remain alone at Bregenz; he returned to his friend at Arbon, the priest Willimar, to whom he related the sudden departure of Columbanus and the punishment he so unjustly inflicted on him. Willimar poured the oil of consolation into the wounded heart of Gall and raised his drooping spirit with the promise of every possible assistance. He moreover charged his two clerics, Maginald and Theodore, to nurse the abandoned monk during his illness. Through the kindness of Willimar and the care of his clerics, St. Gall regained his health and strength. "O, blessed illness," exclaims Walfried Strabo, "stronger than any human strength and better than health! Like his divine Lord, St. Gall became sick that by the preaching of the heavenly word he might cure our souls. He was not enabled to undertake the journey with his master that he might lead us in the path of virtue and truth."

Having completely recovered, St. Gall wished to retire to a solitary place. Taking for his guide a deacon, named Hildebold, an expert in hunting and fishing, he left Arbon to seek a spot where he might build a cell. They went into the wilderness, in the Swiss Alps, inhabited by bears, wolves, boars and venomous snakes. When evening came, they halted at a place where the river Steinach hollows a bed for itself in the rocks. Throwing their nets into the river they caught some fish, then prepared their scanty supper. After the frugal meal, Gall, desiring to be alone, went deeper into the woods, when his foot was caught in the brushwood and he fell. Hildebold ran to raise him up, but the holy man replied in words of the Psalmist: "Here let me rest; this place have I chosen to be my dwelling-place forever." Prostrate upon the ground he prayed for some time. Then rising up he made a cross of two hazel boughs and fastening it into the earth, he attached it to a reliquary which he carried around his neck, and which contained relics of the Blessed Virgin, of St. Desiderius and St. Mauritius, and he thus prayed : "Lord Jesus Christ, Creator of the world, who hast redeemed the human race by the Holy Cross, grant that this place may serve thy glory and the honor of thy Blessed Mother and all the Saints."

During the night, as Gall was praying, a bear descended from the mountains to collect the remnants of the supper. Gall ordered the beast to bring some wood for a fire. The bear obediently brought him a large piece of dry wood, and Gall rewarded this service with a loaf of bread from his wallet, but he commanded the bear to withdraw from the valley and to retire to the mountains and never to harm man or beast.

Menzel says that Gall once extracted a thorn from the paw of a bear and the animal was so grateful for it that it became a faithful servant and companion of the Saint. The fact is that St. Gall has always been represented with a bear at his side, and that the canton of St. Gall has the figure of a bear on its coat of arms.

In the morning, Hildebold went fishing for their breakfast. As he threw his net, he saw two demons in the form of women on the opposite side of the river. They threw stones at him, shouting : " You have led into this desert that wicked and zealous

man, who has always overcome us." Gall appeared
and banished them away by his prayer: " O, Lord
Jesus Christ, Son of God, do thou command that
these demons leave this place which henceforth may
be sacred to thy holy name." Soon the demons
were heard in the distance weeping and crying out:
" What shall we do? Where shall we go? This
stranger drives us not only from the dwellings of
man, but hunts us even from the lonely desert." Gall
consecrated the place by special prayers and a fast
of three days. He erected an oratory and built
cells for himself and for those who joined him. He
also began to labor at the conversion of his heathen
neighbors to whom he proved his heavenly mission
by many miracles.

Our divine Lord told his disciples that if they
had a lively faith they could expect an unlimited
co-operation of God's omnipotence: " If thou canst
believe, all things are possible to him that believeth."
The strong faith of Gall relied on the power of the
Almighty, and he was not confounded.

Duke Gunzo of Alemania having heard of the
power of miracles given to Gall, sent a letter, be-
seeching him to come and to heal his beautiful and
only daughter Friedeburga who was possessed by
an evil spirit. The Saint refused to comply with
the wishes of Gunzo and disappeared into the mountains of Rhaetia. At Grabs (Quadraves) he met
the pious Deacon John who pressed him to stay at
his house. His retreat was soon discovered, and he
finally consented to go to the ducal castle of Ueber-

lingen. He found Friedeburga lying in her mother's lap, her eyes closed, her mouth wide open, and breathing forth sulphurous odors. St. Gall knelt in fervent prayer, and laying his blessed hand on her head he commanded the demon to depart from the girl. She opened her eyes, rose up and was cured. In gratitude to God for her recovery, Friedeburga, though bethrothed to Sigibert, the eldest son of king Thierry, consecrated her virginity to her divine bridegroom and advised by St. Gall entered a convent. King Sigibert, though sadly disappointed, praised her choice and willingly offered her to the service of God.

Abbot Strabo gives the romantic story in his life of St. Gall. After Friedeburga was completely restored to health, she was sent by her father to the court of king Sigibert at Metz, to whom she was betrothed.

Preparations were made for a gorgeous wedding-feast, but when the fixed day came, Frideburga asked seven days respite to recover her strength. When Sigibert consented, she took advantage and fled to the church of St. Stephen, covered herself with a nun's veil, took hold of the corner of the altar and besought the first champion of the crucified to intercede for her with God that she might remain a virgin. The king was informed of this ; he took the bridal robe and crown which was waiting in the palace for his affianced and with his noblemen he entered the church. The princess was terrified at his appearance and held closer to the altar. But

the king said with a loud voice : " Be not afraid ;
I have come here to do thy will." A priest led her
from the altar to the king who had her arrayed
in her bridal garment, and then placed the royal
diadem over her veil, and after gazing a few moments on his beautiful bride, he said to her : "Such
as thou art here, adorned for my bridal, I yield thee
to the bridegroom whom thou preferrest to me—to
my Lord Jesus Christ." And taking her hand in his,
he laid both hands on the altar giving her up to God.
He left the church, weeping and mourning the love
which he renounced for the sake of the Eternal
Spouse.

Duke Gunzo offered rich presents to the holy
man which he declined ; he was pleased, however,
at the letter which Gunzo sent to the prefect of
Arbon instructing him to assist Gall in the construc-
tion of monasteries and churches.

Gall returned to his place of solitude, and devoted
himself especially to building. One early morning he called his Deacon, Maginald, and asked him
to prepare the altar and sacred vestments, as he
wished to say mass for the repose of the soul of
Columbanus, who had departed from the earth during
the night. He sent Maginald to Bobbio to inquire
about the last moments of his master's holy life.
Maginald returned with a letter from the monks of
Bobbio, relating the particulars of the death of their
abbot and founder. With this letter was sent the
staff of Columbanus which he had bequeathed to
Gall as a sign of forgiveness. This staff of Columba-

nus was devoutly received and reverently preserved. At the time of St. Notker, in the ninth century, it hung over the altar of St. Gall, in the Church of the Monastery. St. Notker took it down one night to beat the devil, who appeared to him in form of a dog, and he used it so vigorously that it had to be repaired by the tinsmith.

St. Gall wrote to the Deacon John, whose hospitality and friendship he had enjoyed at Grabs, inviting him to join his zealous band. John came and placed himself under the guidance of St. Gall, who instructed him for three years in philosophy and the Sacred Scriptures.

A letter came from Duke Gunzo requesting our Saint to attend the election of a bishop for the see of Constance. Gall, accompanied by his two deacons, John and Maginald, went to Constance, where a large number of prelates and priests were assembled. All eyes were centred on the Irish monk, and he was chosen to fill the vacancy. But the enthusiasm of clergy and people could not move him to accept the dignity. "All the good things you have said of me," he remarked, "apply to the Deacon John, whom I have brought with me and whom I now propose as your bishop and father, giving security that he will be a worthy prelate." John was elected against his will and immediately consecrated bishop of Constance. Gall remained with his former pupil for seven days, giving him counsel and instruction for the government of his diocese and encouraging him to an apostolic life. At the bishop's first Pontifical

Mass Gall preached the sermon, still preserved, which inflamed the hearts of his hearers and called from their lips the exclamation: "The Holy Ghost speaks through Gall!" He then retired to his cherished solitude with the blessing of the new bishop.

After some years, a deputation of six Irish monks came from the monastery of Luxeul, and in the name of their community begged him to become their abbot. But he who refused the mitre, now refused the government of the great abbey.

Worn out with labor and years, Gall doubled his prayers and vigils as he felt his death approaching. His old friend, Father Willimar, visited him and entreated him to preach at Arbon on the solemn feast of St. Michael. For the last time, St. Gall addressed the Word of God to the faithful at Arbon, September 29, 640. He was seized with his final illness at Willimar's house, where, on the 16th of October, he breathed his beautiful soul into the hands of his Maker, being in the ninety-fifth year of his age.

When the sad news reached Constance, Bishop John was filled with grief and at once hastened to Arbon and to the house of Willimar. The coffin of the dear departed was opened, and throwing himself on it, the heart-broken bishop exclaimed in pitiful accents: "O, father, my father, why doest thou leave me orphaned and forsaken?" The body was carried to the church where Bishop John sang the Requiem for the soul of his beloved master. The funeral took place at the spot which he had selected to be his resting-place forever, and which bears to

the present day the blessed name of St. Gall.
Wonderful in life, St Gall became even more glo-
rious after his death by the number of miracles
wrought at his intercession and by the fruits of his
heroic labors. " When he died," Montalembert remarks," the entire country of the Alamans had become
a Christian province, and round his cell were already
collected the rudiments of the great monastery
which, under the same name of St. Gall, was to become one of the most celebrated schools of Christen-
dom, and one of the principal centres of intellectual
life in the Germanic world."

CHAPTER V.

S T. SIGISBERT was one of the twelve Irish monks who left their native land with the great Columbanus, and with him were expelled from France. Following him to Germany, Sigisbert finally settled at Dissentis, in a vast solitude at the foot of Mount St. Gothard, where, near a fountain he built a cell of branches. The pagan inhabitants of this bleak and lonely region first admired the noble stranger and listened with pleasure to his eloquent plea for the Crucified God, but when he attempted to cut down an oak tree which they regarded as holy to their gods, one of them aimed an axe at his head. Sigisbert made the sign of the cross and disarmed his assailant. The work of conversion proceeded slowly. Among the converts was a wealthy man, St. Placidus, who suffered martyrdom in 630. Assisted by him Sigisbert built a monastery, the first in German Switzerland, and still existing. Disciples gathered around him. At the outset they followed the rule of Columbanus, for which, however, they afterwards substituted the rule of St. Benedict.

The monastery of Dissentis became the mother of many sainted prelates and martyr-priests. It is an

interesting and pleasing fact for Irish Catholics that
an Irish monk won and sanctified with his illustrious
life and heroic works the very source of the River
Rhine, which takes its rise near Dissentis, where the
mountains are capped with eternal snow and the
thundering avalanches are proclaiming the infinite
power of that mighty God whom Sigisbert announced
to the inhabitants.

CHAPTER VI.

ST. TRUDPERT.

ABOUT the year 640, a pious old man arrived in the valley which is watered by the little brook Neumagen, south of Freiburg, in the Black Forest. The venerable arrival was an Irish monk, who came here to rest from his long pilgrimages and to prepare himself in this solitude for the journey to the land of eternal peace.

This holy pilgrim was *St. Trudpert*, a brother of Bishop Rupert, of Worms, afterwards the apostle of Bavaria and founder of the church of Salzburg.

No better spot, indeed, could St. Trudpert choose for seclusion and meditation than that lovely valley, surrounded by rugged mountains and clothed with evergreen pines and firs. The pines are the characteristic trees of the Black Forest. They are said to have been sown there by the hand of God. "On their summit God Himself treads, and through their branches rings the sound of which all German poetry is but an echo," says Bayard Taylor. Here, in this overpowering silence of the mighty forest, St. Trudpert prayed and toiled, turning the bleak wilderness into a blooming valley, at the same time weeding from the hearts of the people vice and error and sowing in their souls the seed of eternal life. "In day time busy like Martha, spending the night at the feet of his Master like Mary." (Hefele.)

In honor of the Prince Apostle, St. Peter, at whose tomb he had often knelt in fervent devotion, he erected a chapel and cell, which, since then, have become celebrated throughout southern Germany. Six men assisted him in building and cultivating the soil ; they reluctantly bore his kind reprimands and his exhortations to labor and industry. One afternoon, while exhausted by toil and by the scorching rays of the sun, he lay on a bench under a tree resting his old limbs, one of these wicked servants split the head of his master with an axe, and thus ended the spotless life of the Irish missionary. His sainted body was laid at rest in his own loved chapel of St. Peter, which soon became the celebrated shrine for devout pilgrimages. A large Benedictine monastery was erected on the hallowed spot, bearing the name of St. Trudpert, whom Abbot Gerbert, in his history of the Black Forest, truly calls the " bright star of the Western Schwarzwald," and his monastery, " the station for Christian missionaries." A monk of St. Trudpert, who wrote in the twelfth century, says of the foundation :   " Watered by the sweat of the holy man, sprinkled with his blood, preserved by his prayers, the monastery remains unto the present day."

CHAPTER VII.

ST. KILIAN AND HIS TWO COMPANIONS.

ST. KILIAN, the son of an Irish nobleman, is honored as the Apostle of Franconia, or northern Bavaria. According to the custom of that time, his pious parents sent their promising boy to a monastery where he would be trained in the fear and knowledge of God. Young Kilian grew in sanctity and learning and became a model priest and monk of the Benedictine Order. One day when meditating in his cell on those words of our blessed Lord,—"If any one will come after me, let him deny himself, take up his cross and follow me,"—Kilian was seized with such a desire to suffer for his Master's cause that he resolved to become a missionary to a heathen nation. He left his native shore with eleven companions, and having safely landed in France, the Spirit of God directed his steps across the Rhine to the south of Germany. He reached Würzburg, in Franconia, a charming place, surrounded by softly-sloping hills. On one of these hills, Kilian with his two companions, Colonat the priest and Totnan the deacon, planted the saving cross of the blessed Redeemer, from which fact the hill bears the name of Kreuzberg (Mount of the Cross) to the present day.

The inhabitants, the ancient Franks, were given to war and plunder. They dressed in skins of animals, lived in gloomy forests and followed the chase. They worshipped Hulda, the goddess of hunting, to whom they offered cruel sacrifices, even of human beings. And yet our Irish missionaries were pleased with the people and the country. Kilian's old biographer (who wrote about the year 800) records the Saint's impression : " Brethren, how beautiful is this country, how cheerful are its people ; and still they are in the darkness of error." The Saint and his companions studied the language and customs of the nations, and then proposed to make a journey to Rome, in order to obtain the sanction of the Vicar of Christ before entering upon the rich harvest which they saw before them. "If it be the will of God," Kilian said, " when we shall have received the sanction of the Apostolic See, we shall, under its guidance, return again to this people, and preach to them the name of our Lord Jesus."

" Without delay," the old chronicler adds, "their deeds corresponded with their words, and they set out for the threshold of St. Peter, the prince of the Apostles. On arriving there, the holy Pope John had already passed to his eternal rest ; but they were lovingly and honorably welcomed by his successor, Pope Conon. And this holy pontiff, having heard whence and for what motive they had come, and to what country they were desirous to devote themselves with such ardour, received their profession of

our holy faith." After having convinced himself
that their faith was pure and their purpose single, he
consecrated Kilian a bishop, and then commissioned
the three holy men "in the name of God and St.
Peter to teach and preach the Gospel of Christ."

They returned to Würzburg in the winter of 687
and began their blessed work of conversion. Crowds
of people flocked to them eager for the word of God,
and before long a great number of natives received
baptism; among them Theobald, Duke of Franconia, to whom Kilian gave the name of Gozbert.
Soon after, Kilian found out that Gozbert was mar-
ried to Gailana, his sister-in-law. He went to the
duke and fearlessly explained to him that the marriage of a Christian with his wife's sister was invalid.
Gozbert, as if awaking from a heavy dream, an-
swered : "Hard things thou doest preach, O, man of
God, but I will obey thee and leave her for the sake
of Him who gave all for me." Gozbert was about
to proceed on a military expedition, therefore asked
leave to defer the matter until his return. While the
duke was gone to the war, the wicked Gailana, like
the wife of King Herod, brooding revenge and thirst-
ing for the blood of Bishop Kilian and his two companions, hired two barbarians to accomplish her dark
design.

Kilian was informed in a heavenly vision of the
imminent martyrdom. Calling his faithful companions, he said : "Let us prepare for the coming of the
Lord, for he is at the door." On July 8, 689, at the

midnight hour, while the three holy men were praying and recommending their souls into the hands of their Father in heaven, the assassins rushed in upon them and sent their spirits to realms of everlasting joy. Thus died Kilian, the Apostle of Franconia, in defending, like St. John the Baptist, the sanctity of the marriage tie, and with Colonat and Totnan sealed the Gospel they had preached with their blood. Their bodies, together with their sacred vessels, missals, and pontifical vestments, were thrown into a deep pit.

When Gozbert returned from the war and inquired for his spiritual father, he was told that Kilian and his two companions had left the country, but the justice of God soon brought the concealed murder to light. One of the assassins became insane, and ran through the streets of the city in a frenzy, crying out: "O, Kilian, Kilian! how horribly thou dost persecute me. I see the sword, red with thy blood, hanging over my head." He died a most revolting death by tearing his flesh with his teeth. The other assassin killed himself with his own sword. And she who had ordered the impious deed, the wicked Gailana, was continually haunted by terrible visions of her foul crime which drove her into incurable insanity.

The holy remains of the martyrs were carefully raised from the obscure pit and reverently laid in a sacred place until a century later, when Bishop Burkhard gave them a permanent resting-place in the solemn crypt of his cathedral at Würzburg.

Tertullian wrote of the martyrs in his days that their blood was the seed of Christians. The three Irish martys who sprinkled the soil of Franconia with their blood sowed the first seed of Christianity which since then has grown into a mighty tree whose roots have struck so deeply into the earth that the storms of twelve centuries have not shaken it nor torn off its lofty branches.

CHAPTER VIII,

ST. DISIBOD.

ST. DISIBOD was born in Ireland, of rich and pious parents, who lost their wealth through the relentless wrath of a tyrant. They succeeded, however, in giving their son an excellent education. Disibod was ordained priest at the age of thirty years. His noble qualities of heart and mind won for him the mitre, which he wore but a short time, being driven from his bishopric by the snares and persecutions of wicked men. He left Ireland with three companions, Gillidad, Clement and Sallust. Travelling through Germany for ten years, he preached the word of God, converting many from error and vice to the way of truth and virtue. But longing for solitude, he took up his abode on a romantic elevation in the Rhenish Palatinate, now known as Disibodenberg, the mount of St. Disibod, by whose base flow peacefully the rivers Glan and Nahe. He selected this wooded mountain, because it was difficult of access and thus separate from the world below. When the Saint took possession of it, he prayed : " O God who dwellest in the highest and rulest the abysses, grant that the beauty of this place may serve for the beauty of immortal souls."

Here he built cells for himself and his companions, and led a life of mortification and austerity, living on the coarsest fare which the Solitude yielded them.

The lustre of his sanctity soon shone through the darkness of the forest. The people from the neighboring country flocked to the mountain to be instructed and edified by the word and example of Disibod.

Princes and people furnished him with the means for the building of a large monastery where he gathered about him many disciples who followed the strict rule of St. Benedict and vowed themselves to a heremitical life.

God glorified his faithful servant on earth by the power of miracles. The chronicler relates that Disibod gave speech to a dumb man; he cured a man suffering with the falling sickness and cleansed a leper. He possessed the gift of prophecy: he foretold the future trials of his monastery and the near approach of his death. The mountain, from which the traveller gains a magnificent view over the surrounding vine-clad hills and fertile valleys, became illustrious on accout of the virtues of the Saint who died here at the age of eighty-one years, on the 8th day of July, in the latter half of the seventh century, and was buried on the mountain. A sweet, heavenly fragrance lingered around the body and the grave of the saint for thirty days, and many miracles nourished the veneration and devotion to Disibod.

His life was written by St. Hildegard in the year 1179, at the command of Helinger, abbot of Disibodenberg. In the century following his death his body was raised by St. Boniface and deposited in the church of the monastery.

Though the years of his birth and of his death are unknown, yet the name and work of St. Disibod will never be forgotton in German lands where many altars containing particles of his precious relics are erected to perpetuate the pious memory of the Irish hermit.

CHAPTER IX.

ST. VIRGILIUS.

THE sons of St. Patrick illumined the Church of Ireland not only with the splendors of their sanctity, but also with the brightness of their learning and scholarship. Among the most learned men of the eighth century we mention St. Virgilius, in Irish, Feargal or O'Farrell, who like many of his countrymen left his native land to work as a missionary in a foreign country. He appeared at the court of France about the year 743, and was kindly received by Pepin, then mayor of the palace, who became greatly interested in the learned Irish priest, and recommended him to Otto, Duke of Bavaria. After a few years of apostolic work in Bavaria, Virgilius was appointed abbot of St. Peter's monastery at Salzburg.

A discussion arose between himself and St. Boniface as to the rebaptizing of persons, baptized by a certain priest who used ungrammatical latin. The case was referred to Rome and decided against Boniface.

Again, he was brought before the court of Rome in a controversy which revealed the depths of his astronomical learning. Virgilius held that the earth was not flat like a sheet of water, but spherical or ball-shaped; he was the first who proved the existence of antipodes or of people living under the earth. It appears that Boniface was ill-informed regarding the teaching of Virgilius, and that he probably misrepresented, though unintentionally, the case of the abbot of Salzburg, stating to the Holy See that Virgilius taught the existence of other worlds and other nations, yet to be saved by a Redeemer. One thing is certain that the disputes of these two eminent Saints were settled without injury to their dignity and to the respect in which they were held by their contemporaries.

Virgilius was elected bishop of Salzburg, in 756, by Pope Stephen II. But the humble monk contrived to defer his consecration for two years, hoping to finally be relieved altogether from the exalted position, and though exercising episcopal jurisdiction, he had his Irish companion Dobda consecrated as auxiliary bishop to perform the necessary episcopal functions in his place. At last he gratified the ardent wishes of the clergy and people and took on himself the episcopal dignity.

He built a Cathedral and consecrated it in honor of St. Peter and St. Rupert. As bishop he continued to observe the monastic rule, and led a most austere and rigorous life. He charged twelve secular priests with the sacred ministry at his Cathedral, whilst he, with a band of zealous monks, his former disciples, travelled through his extensive diocese, preaching the gospel and evangelizing the still pagan districts.

In his apostolic wanderings, Virgilius, with his missionaries, discovered the celebrated springs of Gastein and reopened the famous ore-mountains of Salzburg, thus adding to his spiritual blessings many material and temporal benefits on the people of Salzburg.

Virgilius died November 27, in the year 784, and was canonized in 1233.

CHAPTER X.

IRELAND BROUGHT GERMANY THE ROMAN CATH-OLIC FAITH.

INFIDEL and anti-Catholic writers have not hesi-tated to assert that St. Patrick established a Church in Ireland independent of the See of Peter; and that his teaching essentially differed from that of the Church of Rome. As a consequence, they claim that the Irish missionaries who evangel-ized Germany held no communion with the Vicar of Christ, and that their doctrine was even opposed to the tenets of the Catholic Church. Authentic his-tory, however, tells of the affection and devotion of the early Irish Christians to the See of St. Peter, which their blessed apostle St. Patrick had infused into their hearts.

We find in the early history of the Irish Church how Irish pilgrims flocked to Rome to honor the relics of the apostles and to pay filial reverence to the Vicar of Christ. Germanus the Younger, a contemporary of St. Patrick, visited the shrines of Rome and spent much time in prayer before the tombs of the apostles, shedding tears of joy and consolation, and could only satisfy his reverential ardor by kissing, again and again, the hallowed threshold of St. Peter. St. Enda, the "virginal

saint from Arran Island," the Anthony of the Irish
Church, received Holy Orders in the Eternal City,
before he left Italy; he founded a monastery in the
vicinity of Rome and called it *Lœtium, i. e.,* monastery of heavenly joy. Whilst Enda was in Rome,
the Pope died. The people and clergy assembled
in St. Peter's Church to elect a successor. Enda
was present with his two companions, Ailbe and
Benedict. All were prostrate around the altar when
a dove came flying through the church and alighted
on the shoulder of Benedict. Clergy and people
regarded this as a heavenly sign and elected him
Pope. Nothing, however, could induce the humble
son of St. Patrick to accept the papal dignity. Before St. Enda left Rome, he received the blessing of
the newly elected pontiff, and also a gift of the four
gospels and a chasuble richly wrought in silver and
gold.

Several Irish saints received episcopal consecration
from the hands of the Popes themselves. St. Car-
thage, who sanctified the banks of the Mang with the
purity and zeal of his apostolic life was consecrated
in Rome. St. Laserian studied in Rome, was ordained priest by Pope Gregory the Great, and consecrated bishop by Pope Honorius I.

St. Flannan, "The king of meekness," went to
Rome on a pilgrimage, and, against his wish, was
consecrated first bishop of Killaloe, by the Sovereign
Pontiff himself. Thus we find the early Irish bishops
united in closest bonds with the successors of St.
Peter. The signature of Bishop Sedulius, an Irish-

man, is affixed to the decrees of a Council, held in
Rome, in 721. In the third Lateran Council, an
Irish bishop was interrogated as to his means of sup-
port, and he gave the characteristic reply : " My
whole sustenance depends on three milch cows, and,
according as any one of these becomes dry, another
is substituted by my people."

The pilgrimages of Irish monks and bishops became so numerous and frequent that special hospices
were erected on the Continent for the reception of
Irish pilgrims. Such resting-places were founded
in Cologne, Paris, Ratisbon, Vienna, etc. The
ardor of the Irish to visit the relics of the apostles is
characterized in history as insatiable.

Cardinal Moran writes : " Thus were reciprocally
bound together the churches of Ireland and Rome :
Rome was famed in Ireland as being the Apostolic
See, and hence our saints went on pilgrimages to
venerate the Vicar of Christ, and pay their vows at
the shrines of the Apostles. Ireland, too, famed in
Rome, her religious perfection, and sanctity and
skill in sacred science won the admiration of the
faithful of the Holy City ; and when their own monasteries were laid waste and their sanctuaries pillaged
by ruthless invaders, we find them seeking a sacred
asylum in Ireland, in whose hallowed retreat they
might pursue undisturbed the highest paths of spiritual perfection."

We cannot conclude this chapter without translat-
ing a description of Ireland given, in the ninth
century by the learned German monk Ermenrich

in his address to Grimald, abbot of St. Gall : " We have it from ancient authors that St. Columbanus, St. Gall and their companions came hither to convert the pagan barbarians to the faith of Christ.

How could we ever forget the isle of Erin, from whence the sun of faith, the radiance of so great a light has risen for us ! Though born in a country towards the East, yet, we receive the light of faith from the far West, from the utmost bounds of the earth, from whence also this light has shone upon other nations.

Ireland is rich, adorned with the rarest gifts of nature, but she excels yet more by the most extraordinary gifts of grace. There, winter is so mild that the snow remains upon the ground scarcely for three days. What nature shows in figure is realized spiritually in the Irish Church ; for, to her apply the words of Holy writ : "She shall not fear for her house in the cold of snow ; for all her domestics are clad in double garments." Her teachers are clothed with the mantle of the old and the new Testaments, equipped with pure faith and good works, filled with the love of God and of their neighbor, therefore, she shall not fear that her household perish in the cold of snow, which falls upon the earth through infidelity, heresy and schism.

No snake nor other venemous creature can live on that island ; in like manner, no one can be in communion with the Irish church, who, infected with heresy, tries to poison others. And when such false prophets (teachers) come to Ireland from other countries to unite themselves to the church of Ireland they shall be immediately destroyed by the breath of the doctors of faith, that is to say, they will either be expelled or converted; for the Irish fathers of the church are like the doctrine of the apostle, to the one an odor of life, to the other an odor of death.

In Ireland the bark of the trees and all the plants resist any kind of poison, just as the word of God, carried from there all over the world, removes the corruptions of Satan and pours into the wounds of men the balm of eternal salvation.

Erin flows with milk and honey; and her church abounds in the milk of heavenly doctrine and in the honey of wisdom, which she industriously prepares for high and low; and as her sunny hills are crowned with purple vines and clustering grapes so does her church glitter in the blood of her martyrs. The countless birds, deer and goats remind us of her innumerable saints, who have soared to God or who have so excelled in prudence or strength of soul as to have overcome the temptations of Satan and escaped his snares of sin. In fact the church of Ireland is a faithful (true) picture of the Catholic Church, which, in the midst of the ocean of time, is assailed by the attacks of devils, exposed to the storms of godlessness and the persecutions of the wicked, but being built on the rock, Jesus Christ, she will endure forever. Her pilot is God, her rowers the apostles of Christ, and their successors, the bishop and abbot. Such oarsmen were St. Columbanus and St. Gall, who went out from that

corner of the earth and came to us, as also **did**
that holy martyr of Christ, St. Boniface, who came
from the same place to bring to our beloved father-
land the light of faith.   And all, who faithfully follow these blessed apostles, will be safely led into
the haven of eternal rest."

www.ingramcontent.com/pod-product-compliance
Lightning Source LLC
Chambersburg PA
CBHW031814090426
42739CB00008B/1267